OOPS!

Louis Phillips

illustrated by Doug Jamieson

☆ ☆ ☆ ☆ ☆

BEAUFORT BOOKS, INC. ❧ NEW YORK ❧ TORONTO

Library of Congress Cataloging in Publication Data
Phillips, Louis. Oops!
1. Errors—Anecdotes, facetiae, satire, etc. I. Title.
PN6231.E74P5   818′.5402   81-18088
ISBN 0-8253-0080-0   AACR2

Published in the United States by Beaufort Books, Inc., New York.
Published simultaneously in Canada by General Publishing Co. Limited

Printed in the United States of America   First Edition
10 9 8 7 6 5 4 3 2 1
Designer: Victoria Gomez

The author gratefully acknowledges the following newspapers, publications, wire services, and various offices for granting kind permissions to reprint certain material herein: United Press International, *Time, Reader's Digest,* Associated Press, *The Washington Post, The New York Daily News, The New York Post, The New York Times, The St. Louis Post-Dispatch, The Hartford Courant, Films in Review* (for "Cinemistakes" by Edward Connor), The National Safety Council, and Random House (for selections from *An Open Book* by John Huston). The author wishes also to extend thanks to the following individuals: Ms. Ivy Fischer-Stone, Mr. Charles Hunt, Ms. Fifi Oscard, Ms. Toni Dorfman, and Ms. Susan Suffes.

This book is dedicated to the Pinwheel Writers

       Lou
       Bob "the Pearl"
       Michael
       Patricia
       Terry
       Paulette

for that time when everything went right

Extra! Extra! Read all about it (right here in OOPS!):

A MAN RECEIVES A MILLION DOLLAR CHECK BY MISTAKE
PRESIDENT TRUMAN DEDICATES AN AIRPORT
TO THE WRONG PERSON
THE DAY JIM MARSHALL OF THE MINNESOTA VIKINGS
RAN THE WRONG WAY
FRED MERKLE'S FAMOUS BONEHEAD PLAY

& much much more.

The purpose of this light-hearted romp through heartbreak, triviality, and coincidence is to provide all of us mistake-makers with some inexpensive therapy. After browsing through this collection of boners, slips, errors, miscues, bobbles, bloopers, malapropisms, blunders, stupidities, etc., you should feel better about yourself. Why should we allow guilt about our blunders to ruin our day?

I myself have only made one small error. I wrote this book when I should have been outside in the sun. I will now place such foolishness behind me and move on, I hope, to bigger and better things. So shall you, after you have bought this book and have studied it closely.

Forgive yourself. Enjoy. As ex-king Alfonso said, "A King can make mistakes."

Louis Phillips
1982 or thereabouts

❧ | ERRATA

Page 21 should be page 46.

Wrong Way Corrigan might have deliberately crossed the Atlantic Ocean. Since he filed a flight plan for Los Angeles, he might have claimed to have made a mistake in order to keep from losing his pilot's license.

Some experts feel that OOPS should be spelled OOOPS. The illustrator suggests WHOOPS! Hula wants HOOPS. The Greeks prefer OPS. Do not write the publishers. They have moved to a new location.

JOHN UNITAS, who played with the Baltimore Colts from 1956 to 1969, is one of the greatest football players of all time. Even so, John Unitas holds the record for the most fumbles committed in a lifetime—eighty-four fumbles.

There! Don't you feel better?

❦ | IT PAYS TO PHONE AHEAD

"Roseau, Minnesota: Without sending word ahead, Seter Gavelin left for Sweden to see his brother, Ihren Gavelin. Simultaneously, Ihren sailed on a surprise visit to the United States. Seter is now in Sweden; Ihren, in Minnesota."

Newsweek (July 25, 1938)

❦ | TRUMAN, UNBRIEFED, DEDICATES AIRPORT TO WRONG PERSON

Girl killed in plane was to be honored, not war flyer

Carey, Idaho. June 9, 1948—President Truman made a slip here yesterday and dedicated an airport to a flyer killed in the war, instead of to a girl killed at home while hedge-hopping with a boyfriend.

Truman had left Sun Valley in such a hurry he had not been briefed properly on what he was to say at Carey. He knew he was to dedicate an airport and when he drove up he was welcomed by a group of war veterans, whereupon he launched into a speech dedicating the airport to the memory of a flyer.

Carey had the flags flying, a big welcome banner across its only street, and a wreath and microphone ready. The President dedicated the field from the back seat of his open car. He said he was happy to be able to present this wreath to the mother and father of this boy who died that "liberty and his country" might live.

After he had finished his little speech, someone whispered in his ear that the airport was being dedicated not to a war pilot, but to the memory of Wilma, sixteen-year-old daughter of Mr. and Mrs. Sheldon Coates.

"I'm sorry I made a mistake," the President apologized to the girl's mother. "Oh, that's all right," she said.

St. Louis Post-Dispatch

✵ | SOME MISTAKES REALLY BURN US UP

Back in the middle of the eighteenth century a huge fireworks display was held in London to commemorate the peace of Aix-La-Chappelle, ending the war between Britain and France and other European countries. Unfortunately, the fireworks got a bit out of hand: three people died in accidents at the scene, and several royal buildings caught fire. Numerous persons were severely injured.

P.S. This was the fireworks display for which George Frederick Handel wrote his "Music for the Royal Fireworks."

✷ | AND OF COURSE ALEXANDER HAIG HAS BEEN KNOWN TO MAKE MISTAKES

On August 6, 1981, Secretary of State Alexander Haig, Jr. was briefing reporters about talks that had taken place between President Reagan and Egypt's President Anwar Sadat. At one point in his talk, he accidentally referred to Reagan as President Nixon. When he realized that he had made a mistake, he blurted out, "Did I just say . . . Oh my God!"

Then, to compound the error, Mr. Haig added: "I was looking ahead."

Secretary of State Alexander M. Haig, Jr. has been involved in another boo-boo. It seems he was at the state dinner at the White House to honor Japan's prime minister, and among the guests was Sen. Spark Matsunaga, D-Hawaii. At cocktails before dinner Matsunaga and his wife suddenly had the feeling something was a bit strange. "My wife and I kept wondering why in the world, when I'd talk to Sen. Jackson or someone, an aide would escort us back to the Japanese," Matsunaga said. Then before the start of the dinner and the arrival of President Reagan, the Japanese and American guests were escorted into separate waiting rooms. Matsunaga, a native-born American of Japanese ancestry, was herded into the waiting room with the Japanese. Haig, the only other American in the room, made his way through the assembled Japanese introducing himself. Then he welcomed Matsunaga to the United States. Matsunaga put on his best Japanese accent, and told Haig it had been his pleasure to vote for his confirmation in the Senate. "You should have seen his face," Matsunaga said.

People in the News by R. E. Krieger
Hartford Courant (July 5, 1981)

✺ | WHY OFFICIALS WRING HANDS

Salt Lake City, Utah. January 8, 1954 (AP)—While loading a bag with clothes to be sent to fire victims in Pusan, Korea, Mrs. Albert Ehlert lost a diamond ring. She asked authorities of the Clothes For Korea Drive to search for her ring.

The Army at the post in Stockton, California, offered to search through 175,-000 pounds of clothing with a metal detector. A twenty-ton semi-trailer loaded with clothes was combed thoroughly.

Today Mrs. Ehlert found the ring—in her kitchen cupboard.

Now drive officials are trying to find the owners of two other rings found during the search.

❧ | PEOPLE HAVE BEEN KNOWN
TO MAKE MISTAKES IN THEIR SLEEP

Dived From Window in Sleep
Girl Dreaming of a Practice Swim Has Her Nose Broken in Fall

Bayport, Long Island.—Miss Marion Sheridan, who is spending the summer here is fond of bathing, and since the water became warm enough for the sport she has never allowed a day to pass without taking a dip in the bay. Last night, so she told friends later, she fell asleep dreaming of the swim which she would take this morning.

She had intended to go down to the end of the pier and practice a new dive, and so realistic did the dream become that the young woman arose in her sleep and threw herself out of the second story window of her home.

She was found at daybreak, lying unconscious on the grass. Physicians were summoned, and when they had revived the young woman, she told of her dreams. They found that she had escaped with a broken nose.

The New York Times, (July 5, 1908)

9

✥ | WHEN MAKING MISTAKES THERE'S NO PLACE LIKE HOME

It was the 4th game of the 1941 world series, and the Yankees were battling the Dodgers. With two out in the top of the 9th, the Yankees trailed the Bums by the score of four to three. Tommy Heinrichs was batting for the Yankees, and, with two strikes against him, Heinrichs swung at a curve-ball and missed. The game was over. The Dodgers had won. But wait . . . Dodger catcher Mickey Owen dropped the third strike and Heinrichs reached first base. With Heinrichs on first, Joe DiMaggio stepped into the batter's box and singled. Charley Keller came to bat and banged out a double. Bill Dickey walked. Joe Gordon doubled, and the Yankees went on to win by the score of seven to four.

That dropped third strike ranks with the all-time great errors in baseball history.

❧ | METER MATTER

In 1915, Charles Steinmetz wrote in *Ladies' Home Journal* that electricity could be made available so cheaply that "it will not pay to install meters."

❧ | HOWEVER

There is a popular conception that lightning never strikes twice in the same place. This is most definitely an error. Lightning often strikes the same place—even more than twice.

*

Even Xaveria Hollander (the "Happy Hooker") can make mistakes. In *Forum* magazine she stated, "I've had friends and lovers from most of the ranking United Nations, and I hope to be a member of the welcoming committee for our first extraterritorial visitors."

We hope she meant *extraterrestrial visitors.*

"I never made a mistake in my life; at least, never one that I couldn't explain afterwards."

Rudyard Kipling

*

Tennis star Martina Navratilova tells her fans how difficult it was for her to learn English:

> "I made some mistakes along the way. Once I was trying to say 'It's no skin off my nose,' and I said instead, 'It's no hair off my chest.'"

13

🏴 | 3,500-MILE HIKERS WIND UP IN WRONG TOWN FOR TALKS

East Hampton, Connecticut. April 14, 1951 (UPI)—Mr. and Mrs. William Stockdale, who walked 3,500 miles across the United States without getting lost, were slated to discuss their cross-country jaunt at a local church last night. Some 125 persons waited for their arrival almost an hour.

The group broke up when it was learned the Stockdales had gone to the town of Hampton, 30 miles east of here, by mistake.

THE LAWYER WHO GOT CAUGHT FOR SPEEDING

London, England. November 14, 1952 (UPI)—George Jones, a lawyer, couldn't find his driver's license when a policeman stopped him for speeding.

Just after Jones was given a summons and the cop had left, Jones found his license. He sped after the policeman, but was stopped by another for speeding.

Jones was fined one pound for the first offense, and two pounds for the second.

SAFETY INSTRUCTOR BACKFIRES

Lawrenceville, Virginia. 1951—Dr. C. A. Thomas, local dentist, addressed a study group on safety in the use of firearms. On his way home, Dr. Thomas bought a BB rifle to use in chasing off dogs that had been getting into garbage cans. The rifle failed to work, so Dr. Thomas returned the weapon and demonstrated its failings to the store clerk.

The rifle suddenly discharged, and another doctor was quickly called to remove the BB pellet that had lodged itself in Dr. Thomas's finger.

⚓ | SENATOR ADDRESSES LEGISLATURE.
TURNS OUT TO BE A MENTAL PATIENT

Columbus, Ohio. April 14, 1951—Embarrassed Ohio Legislators learned last night that a visiting "Maine State Senator" who addressed both houses of the legislature actually was a fugitive from a mental hospital.

The speeches were delivered last Wednesday. The invitation to make them was part of the courtesy the Legislature accords visiting dignitaries.

The man, Paul Snow, 34 years old, of Biddeford, Maine, escaped last Monday from the Veterans' Hospital in Chillicothe, Ohio. Now he is being held in the Fairfield County jail at Lancaster, Ohio.

Discovery of his identity came when a publicity man attempted to reach him through a Maine newspaper.

Snow visited the Legislature Tuesday and said that he was interested in Ohio's sales tax. Legislators said he appeared well acquainted with taxation measures. They invited him to sit in on a meeting of the Senate Taxation Committee.

Wednesday he was invited to address both houses of the Republican dominated Legislature. In the Senate, he gave a bitter tongue-lashing directed at Democrats in general. (Snow said that he was a Republican.)

Both Democratic and Republican legislators were embarrassed. Usually a visiting dignitary confines his remarks to those of a non-controversial nature.

17

HOW NOT TO EXTERMINATE RATS

Detroit, Michigan. Ingmar Iverson, in a hospital here, is not so sure he has found a successful method of exterminating rats.

Iverson poured a can of gasoline-oil mixture into a rat hole and struck a match. He was taken to the hospital with severe burns on his left leg. Firemen put out the blaze before there was any property damage.

The rats could not be reached for comment.

DOES THIS RING A BELL?

In the movie *Five Graves to Cairo*, there is a scene that shows a hotel in the Libyan Desert. On the wall of the hotel is a sign, written in Arabic, that tells travellers to ring the hotel bell for service.

This is a mistake.

In Libya, the ringing of bells is forbidden to Arabs.

❦ | BEER BARES ALL

Jack Ruppert was a well-known brewer. He was also one of the early owners of the New York Yankees, and when the Yankee games were broadcast on the air, Rupert's Beer would often be the sponsoring agent. During one game, a radio broadcaster announced to all the Yankee fans, "Boopert's Rear is on the air!"

❦ | FIREMEN GOOF, BLAZE LEVELS 16 BUILDINGS

Stockholm, Sweden (AP)—A raging fire, set by mistake by the local fire-brigade, destroyed 16 houses and barns today in Varnhem, a small farming community in southwestern Sweden.

The fire brigade had been asked by a Varnhem farmer to burn down an old, useless barn. But because of dry weather and a strong wind the fire rapidly spread beyond control and turned the peaceful village into an inferno.

No human casualties were reported, but the damage was estimated at 10 million kronor, about $2.3 million.

In 1631, an edition of the King James Bible published in London printed one of the Ten Commandments to read as "THOU SHALT COMMIT ADULTERY."
    This edition became known as the "Wicked Bible."

✿ | HOW NOT TO DO IT!

Enderlin, North Dakota. March 10, 1951 (UPI)—A Soo Line Railroad movie on employee safety didn't help Carl Nelson. As he stepped from the rail coach where the movie was shown, he fell and broke his leg.

✿ | MONDALE'S SLIP

Cincinnati, Ohio. (UPI)—Vice President Walter Mondale slipped on Sen. Edward Kennedy's name last night, referring to the other half of the Carter-Mondale ticket as "President Kennedy."

Arriving here, he was asked whether he would support Kennedy if the senator got the nomination. "If President Kennedy runs, and I expect him to run, he will be nominated and I am convinced reelected, so we won't have that problem."

Despite Every Precaution They Occur In Even the Best of Films
by Edward Connor

When Ann Sheridan and Richard Carlson, baby-sitting for friends, hear the baby cry in *Winter Carnival* (1939), they go into the nursery to see what is wrong. Carlson bends over the crib and the baby grabs his tie and won't let go. So Miss Sheridan scissors the tie off below the knot, leaving the greater portion in the baby's hand. The baby stops crying, the couple re-emerge in the living room, and—lo and behold!—Mr. Carlson's tie is whole.

Such boners, despite considerable efforts to prevent them, are not infrequent in movies, as observant fans know. Their most common cause is the fact that movies are not photographed in the continuity in which they are written. Which is to say, director, actor, and script girl go ahead with a scene without learning what precedes it in the script.

The most common cinemistakes deal with time.

Time stands absolutely still in *When You're in Love* (1937). The marriage of Grace Moore to Cary Grant is announced by a shot of front page headlines. Later their divorce is similarly reported. However, the news items surrounding the two announcements are identical.

Time is speeded up in *Whom the Gods Destroy* (1934) and *Kid Galahad* (1937). In the former, Robert Young leaves the theatre after the final curtain of the premiere of his new play, goes upstairs to his office—in the same building— and finds the critics' reviews of the play in the morning papers waiting for him on his desk. In *Kid Galahad* Bette Davis comes out of the stadium where Wayne Morris has *just* defeated the world champion and finds in the lobby a picture of Wayne above the inscription: "Kid Galahad, the World's Champion."

Time is pulverized in *Dangerous Mission* (1954). After some of the principals have an early supper, Victor Mature reminds Piper Laurie of a date they have that night. Thereupon a forest fire is reported and the men go off to fight it—in a lengthy sequence in which some of the fire scenes obviously occur in the dead of night, and the concluding shot of smoldering trees appears to be in the early dawn. Yet when the men return to the hotel, Piper is closing her stand in the hotel for the night and tells Victor she is ready to leave.

Clothes dry in no time at all in some moves. When Lily Pons gets to shore after swimming from the boat in *That Girl from Paris* (1936) her suit is dry and completely in press. Franchot Tone hasn't a drop of water on him after coming in out of pouring rain in *Quality Street* (1937). After a fight in the water with Henry Wilcoxon in *Souls at Sea* (1937), Gary Cooper emerges from the drink— dry.

Wounds heal with incredible rapidity. Gary Cooper, shot in the hand in *The*

General Died at Dawn (1936), shortly thereafter eats with the same hand, which is neither wounded nor even bandaged. Van Heflin takes a vicious beating in *Strange Love of Martha Ivers* (1946). As he crawls out of the ditch where thugs have left him bruised, cut and bleeding, he reaches into his mouth and pulls out pieces of broken teeth. In the very next scene his face is clear and unmarked, his teeth in perfect condition.

Anachronisms abound in films.

Although *The Black Room* (1935) is laid in the early nineteenth century, one scene prominently displays a statue of St. Theresa of Lisieux, the popular "Little Flower" saint, who was born in 1873, died in 1897, and was canonized in 1925.

Orson Welles leaves much Shakespearean text out of his production of *Macbeth* (1948), but inserts a scene in which King Duncan and his men renew their baptismal vows and are led in prayer by the "holy father" (Alan Napier). The prayer, to St. Michael the Archangel, was composed by Pope Leo XIII in 1884.

The joy-buzzer was invented and patented in 1933, but that doesn't prevent Victor McLaglen from using one in 1901 in *This Is My Affair* (1937).

There are dial phones and pinball machines in the New York of 1918 in *They Gave Him a Gun* (1937).

The prehistoric man thawed out of ice in *Return of the Ape Man* (1944) is appropriately clad in animal skins. Plainly visible beneath them, in one shot, is some definitely twentieth century underwear. And though *The Egyptian* (1954) recounts events of thirty-three hundred years ago, there is a vaccination mark on the arm of Bella Darvi, a Babylonian temptress.

Movie-gaffs, in the early days, were often the result of ignorance. Hence the research departments now maintained by all major studios. However, research departments are falliable too—and sometimes uncertain, to say the least.

Thus, is it merely the Chinese influence in *Return of Dr. Fu Manchu* (1930) that causes Jean Arthur to walk down the aisle as a bride *before* her bridesmaids? What is the anthropological reason for Anna Sten getting out of bed in *Nana* (1934) with her shoes on? Why does Henry Fonda, as the priest in *The Fugitive* (1947), administer baptism in an invalid form? Although in most films Apaches scalp their victims, in 20th Century-Fox's *Broken Arrow* (1950) it is stated that Apaches never scalp people—only white men do. In Warner's *Santa Fe Trail* (1940), George Custer—he of the last stand—is shown graduating from West Point. In Warner's *They Died with Their Boots On* (1941) Custer and classmates at West Point are told the Civil War necessitates the interruption of their studies and they will be sent to the front without graduating.

The script girl is supposed to note down facts—especially those relating to the garb and physical appearance of the players—which prevent cinemistakes like that of Richard Carlson's tie. But script girls are as absent-minded as the rest of us. In *Captain Kidd and the Slave Girl* (1954), Eva Gabor twice leaves ship in one dress and steps ashore in another. Claudette Colbert does something similar in *Cleopatra* (1934). At the beginning of that picture she is tied to a pillar in the desert and left to die. She is found, rolled in a carpet, and taken to Julius Caesar. When rolled out of the carpet she is clad in a different outfit.

Hair seems to baffle script girls. Tarzan has been clean-shaven in Hollywood jungles for forty years. Although Jon Hall has no shaving equipment—nor anything else—as he flees from the law in *The Hurricane* (1937), he hasn't a trace of beard. Also beardless are some of the men who accompany Captain Bligh on the long open-boat voyage in *Mutiny on the Bounty* (1935), and some of the prisoners undergoing prolonged torture in *Prisoner of War* (1954). Tony Dexter, however, while awaiting execution in *Captain Kidd and the Slave Girl,* is adorned with a snappy, three-pronged beard only a metropolitan hair stylist could concoct.

Script girls seem unable to cope with actors and actresses when they go for walks. Mary Astor puts on rubbers to go out in the rain in *Return of the Terror* (1934), but returns in rubber boots. Mae Clark arrives at her destination in *This Side of Heaven* (1934) wearing shoes different from those shown when she sets forth. W. C. Fields' cane changes from white to black in the course of a few steps in *Mrs. Wiggs of the Cabbage Patch* (1934). Jean Hersholt starts off in *Heidi* (1937) in a stocking cap and finishes his walk wearing a felt hat with feathers.

Money is another hazard for script girls. Wendy Barrie pays for a 75¢ jar of preserves with *one* coin in *Love on a Bet* (1936), and when Jimmy Cagney forces a crook to return $50 in *Lady Killer* (1933), he receives *two* bills. A character in *King for a Night* (1933) drops a nickel in a payphone, asks for long distance, and gets his number without paying another cent.

Gloves also get beyond script girls. Fred Astaire puts his bare hands in his pockets in *Swing Time* (1936) and removes them with gloves on. Glenda Farrell, sitting at a lunch counter in *The Personality Kid* (1934), takes off both gloves and puts them on the counter, but in the next shot removes a glove from her right hand.

Script girls let marvels occur that the scripts do not call for and that few magicians could duplicate.

Cagney hits Robert Armstrong a terrific blow on the chin in *G-Men* (1935), but when Bob gets up from the floor he has a black eye. After merely looking down Bette Davis' throat in *Of Human Bondage* (1934), Phillips Holmes announces she has lung trouble. Although Ann Sothern puts her suitcase on a chair before entering a phone booth in *Fifty Roads to Town* (1937), she emerges with it in her hand. In *Let's Get Married* (1937), Ralph Bellamy pours himself a glass of water by emptying the contents of a pitcher into a glass. Soon afterward Reginald Denny enters the room, and, to rouse Ralph, pours water on him from the same pitcher. Then, Ida Lupino comes in and has a glass of water from it.

As the boat carrying the principal characters in *The Last of Mrs. Cheney*

(1937) passes the Statue of Liberty, the name on its bow is "Rotterdam." When Robert Montgomery talks to the purser, the ship's name has become "Northampton." Later, when Joan Crawford and Frank Morgan stroll on deck, it is "S. S. Britain." In *Queen Christina* (1933) the wind blows in two directions at the same time. As Garbo stands in the bow of a ship in the closing scene, the sails bellow forward as her hair blows backward. And Fredric March goes in two directions at once in *Death of a Salesman* (1951). Beneath the credits Mr. March is driving across the George Washington Bridge from New Jersey to New York yet when he gets to his home in New York he tells his wife he has gotten only as far as Yonkers.

Script girls, of course, are not the only ones responsible for cinemistakes. The cutter contributes his share, as in *Glamour* (1934), when Constance Cummings and Paul Lukas are shown in a restaurant eating soup. In the next shot the table is clear and Miss Cummings is sipping wine, which could be. In the succeeding shot, however, she is eating soup again. The director of *The Golden Mask* (1954) lets a telegraph pole be seen over the shoulder of an actor standing amid desert ruins.

And there are cinemistakes of such ineptitude that they pass human understanding. Thus, in *Alibi Ike* (1935), a player for the NY Giants comes to bat in a uniform bearing the legend "St. Louis Cardinals." At the end of *Viva Villa* (1934) Wallace Beery is solemnly presented with a medal which he has worn earlier in that film. The dinosaur in *Beast from 20,000 Fathoms* (1953) gets into the middle of a roller coaster without breaking any of its wooden structure. Although the prime gimmick in *The Invisible Man* (1933) is that Claude Rains can't wear clothes because they make him *visible,* his footprints in the snow are not of bare feet but of shoes. In the same picture, when Rains, by throwing switches in a railroad station, causes a train to be switched into an abyss, there is no explanation of why a spur from the main track leads to a precipice. The laboratories in *Bride of Frankenstein* (1935) and *Frankenstein Meets the Wolf-man* (1943) are both blown up by switches being pulled *within* the laboratories.

Finally, though cinemistakes do not occur in a film, they may in its title. It was an *emperor* who cavorted in *The King Steps Out* (1936). The cat is alley-gray in *Case of the Black Cat* (1936). There is nary a raid in *The Great Jesse James Raid* (1953). And no more than two coins are ever cast in *Three Coins in the Fountain* (1954).

Reprinted with permission from *Films in Review,* V (Oct. 1954), pp. 409–412.

SOME DAYS ARE BETTER THAN OTHERS

Long Beach, California. 1951—Here's what happened to Cass Waranius at his chicken specialty shop yesterday.

An automobile leaped from a curb and smashed down twenty-five feet of his fence.

Twelve hours later, another car banged into Waranius' truck parked in front of the store.

Three hours after that, still another car leaped the curb and smashed down the remaining 25 feet of fence.

"Talk about lightning striking twice," Waranius said. "Me it hits three times."

SOME BAYS ARE BETTER THAN OTHERS

Calcutta, India. March 31, 1951 (UPI)—A storm of protest arose today over the draining of millions of gallons of water from a lake at "The Rooftop of the World" because the daughter of the Governor of Assam dropped her diamond ring into it.

Some members of the Assam State Assembly referred to the drainage operation for the object as of "great sentimental value," and "thrilling," even "very romantic" but others said it was too romantic for this Atomic Age.

The ring slipped from the finger of Kumari Premi Jairamdas, daughter of Jairamdas Doulatram, as she was feeding fish in a lake in Slullong. Divers failed to retrieve it. For six days, engineers have been diverting millions of gallons of water into a nearby river. There was even a suggestion that the fish should be passed under an X-ray in case the drained lake disclosed no ring.

We don't know if the ring was ever found, and, frankly, we don't care.

✠ | MOO—OOOPS!

In 1955, in Albuquerque, New Mexico, a convention of dairy farmers elected a dairy Queen of Bernalillo and Sandoval Counties. They discovered afterwards that the young lady was allergic to milk.

✠ | LOOK SHARP, BE SHARP

There is a wide-spread belief that the guillotine was invented by Joseph Guillotin and that the first person to be executed by such a machine (one employing a heavy free-falling blade to decapitate its victims) was none other than the "inventor" himself.

Not so.

The guillotine, invented in the Middle Ages, had long been in use before Joseph Guillotin was ever born. Guillotin merely urged the French people to adopt the instrument for the execution of criminals.

The first guillotine execution in France took place in 1792, and the victim was a common highway robber by the name of Peletier. Death by guillotine is now prohibited.

"In Croyden, England, Vice Admiral Sir John Edgell took a careful second look at his notes, abruptly ending his speech before the Royal Navy Old Comrades Association with a confession: 'By mistake I brought a shopping list my wife gave me.'"

Time (November 15, 1948)

*

Ursula Shipton, born in Yorkshire, England, in 1488, was famous in her lifetime for her predictions. There is, however, one prediction that she made a mistake on. She predicted that the world would come to an end in the year 1881:

> The world to an end shall come
> In Eighteen Hundred and Eighty-one.
>
> You can't be right all the time.
> (Thank goodness.)

✻ | *WHO WAS THAT MASKED MAN?*

Creely, Colorado. 1951—Police called for help in nabbing a peeping tom.

Mrs. Herman Meisner was undressing for bed when she saw the peeper. Two sharp eyes behind a black mask stared through the glass of the front door. She screamed, and her husband called the cops. After their arrival, police had to call men from the city pound to catch the peeper—a nervy raccoon perched on a crossbar of the screen door.

✻ | SOME MISTAKES ARE USEFUL

Blotting paper was discovered by accident. A workman at a paper mill in Berkshire, England, forgot to put in sizing, an essential ingredient in paper-making, and so large quantities of useless paper were produced. The thrifty owner decided not to throw the mistakes away, and soon discovered that paper without sizing was very absorbent, and so he began to market the mistakes as "blotting paper." Until that time, people had used sand to dry ink.

And you thought this wasn't a serious book.

35

☙ | EVEN GREAT FILM DIRECTORS CAN MAKE MISTAKES:

John Huston, in his autobiography *An Open Book,* tells us:

> "... I was sent out to cover a story in Astoria. A worker in a tobacco factory had stuck a knife into another worker, and the victim died. It was an unimportant homicide, as such things go. I was sent out to get the simple facts. I did precisely that, but then I got my notes mixed up. When the story appeared in print, I had the owner of the tobacco factory as the assailant. That ended my connection with the *Graphic.*"

❦ | GREAT FILM DIRECTORS MAKE MORE MISTAKES

"While on Adak, I made friends with Jack Chennault, the son of Claire Chennault of Flying Tiger fame. Jack's fighter planes had just been equipped with cameras which were synchronized with the airplanes' guns so that when the pilot pressed the firing button, the cameras recorded the flight of the bullets to their target. This was a new thing, and no action film had as yet been obtained. The cameras were adjusted to accept black-and-white film, but I convinced Jack he should let us modify them to take color film, and I supervised the operation myself so there would be no slip-ups.

An attack was made, and it was a marvelous success, with heavy dogfighting in the air and a number of Zeros shot down. Everybody was ecstatic. The very first combat film, and in color! I sent it back to the States by special courier to be developed. Word came shortly that the film was absolutely blank. It seems I had forgotten to run out the leader—which was some six feet long—in any of the cameras! That was the biggest boner of my Army career."

John Huston, *An Open Book*

☙ | I STILL WOULDN'T WANT TO BELONG TO A CLUB THAT ACCEPTED ME AS A MEMBER DEPT.

"Boston: Tired of being hit on the face by opponents, Jack Gaines, 30, decided to quit boxing and switch to the mild game of golf. On the first tee, he fanned the ball, socked his nose with the grip end of the club on the follow through and landed unconscious."

Newsweek (August 22, 1938)

*

John Firek, Chicago vegetable hawker, cat-napping on his tenement roof, rolled over the edge, fell three flights down, and plopped unhurt on a truck's canvas top. Friends crowded round with congratulations on his luck. "Lucky?" he scoffed. "Now I've gotta pay for busting that guy's truck-top."

Newsweek (September 29, 1934)

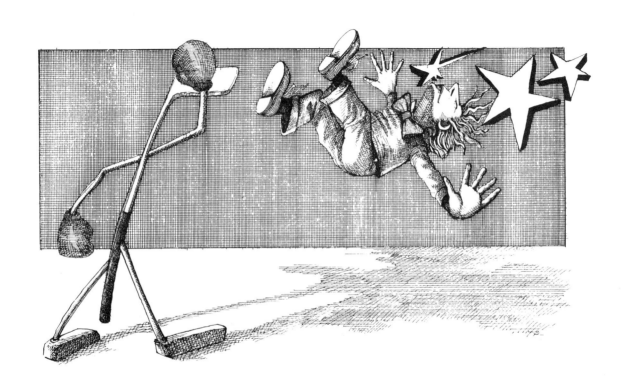

Duxbury, Mass. January 25, 1941 (AP)—Andrew Paanen, 42-years-old, who owns a small cranberry bog, received a $1,000,015.25 check from the government today for complying with the Federal Soil Conservation Program.

Overpaid by exactly one million dollars, because of a treasury check-writer's error, Paanen extracted all the fun he could out of the situation.

He walked into Plymouth National Bank, pushed the check in front of teller Walter Roberts, and calmly asked for cash.

Roberts blinked and raced for the bank executives. They pored over the check, found it valid, and worried about how to provide a million dollars on demand.

Only then did Paanen admit that he was joking. Instead of trying to cash it, he mailed it back to the treasure department to be corrected.

JAPANESE MEN'S FEET TO SPREAD OUT AT LAST

Tokyo, Japan. July 1, 1949 (AP)—No longer will Japanese men's shoes come in only one width—narrow. The custom was originated by imperial decree half a century ago when western dress became formal court attire.

General Douglas MacArthur's headquarters decided that widened lasts* to fit the broad feet of Japanese men should be employed. Hitherto they have cramped their toes inside the narrow width styles or bought shoes far too long to give their feet room.

* Cobbler's term for a wooden mold or form on which shoes are built or repaired.

People once believed that spider webs should be applied to small cuts in order to stop the bleeding. Unfortunately, this remedy often resulted in numerous cases of lockjaw, as the following story from the February 15, 1902, *Boston Evening Transcript* reveals:

> Mrs. Frankland tells of lockjaw having been caused by the application of a cobweb to a slight cut.
>
> 'The wound was a perfectly clean one, and nothing need have resulted from this obedience to a superstitious prejudice had not the cobwebs unfortunately arrested some local germs, and these, getting across the wound, set up the typical symptoms of lockjaw. That this implication of the cobweb was no idle speculation was subsequently proved by portions of the same web, on being inoculated into animals, inducing in the latter well-defined symptoms of tetanus.'
>
> That cobwebs readily catch dust is familiar to everyone who has the mortification of seeing them adorn ceilings and corners. That they also arrest bacteria follows as a natural consequence of dust, and these delicate filaments may become veritable bacterial storehouses.

43

📫 | PHILATELY GETS YOU NOWHERE!

In 1956, the German Republic issued a postage stamp to commemorate the 100th year of Robert Schumann's death. The stamp featured a portrait of the composer against a backdrop of one of his musical scores. Unfortunately, the stamp designer used a score by Schubert (part of Schubert's setting for Goethe's *Wanderer's Nachtlied*). Within days post-office officials, embarrassed by the mistake, withdrew the stamp and replaced Schubert's score with one by Schumann.

In January, 1977, *Esquire* magazine reported the following goof on the part of Marlon Brando and comedian Dick Gregory:

> "Marlon Brando and Dick Gregory flew to Wichita, Kansas, to testify for two American Indians accused of killing F.B.I. agents, but the trial was being held in Cedar Rapids, Iowa."

Oh, well.

⚑ | DO-IT-YOURSELF LAWYER HAS FOOL FOR A CLIENT

Tulsa, Oklahoma. (AP)—Marshall Cummings Jr. has no one but himself to blame for his less-than-successful court appearance.

Cummings, twenty-five, accused of purse snatching, was acting as his own attorney yesterday.

As he cross-examined the victim, he asked her: "Did you get a good look at my face when I took your purse?"

A state jury convicted Cummings of attempted robbery by force and gave him a ten-year prison sentence.

⚑ | PAINTING MISTAKE #45678

In the famous Renaissance painting of the Last Supper reproduced below, the artist depicts oranges being eaten. Oranges were most definitely not served at the Last Supper.

The error came about because Crusaders returning from the Holy Land reported that oranges were growing there, but oranges had not been introduced to the Holy Land until long after Christ's death.

✥ | SYNONYMS FOR MISTAKE

fault

misprint

corrigendum

miscue

blunder

erratum

error

oversight

bungle

slip of the tongue

fallacy

misjudgment

false belief

slip of the pen

misunderstanding

miscalculation

delusion

etc. etc. etc.

There are lots of ways to make mistakes.

In 1953, the State Highway Commission began printing new road maps of the State of Indiana. 40,000 maps had been printed when the Commission discovered that the printer had left out the city of Aurora.

A PREDICTION FOR 1905

A cartoonist for *Life* in 1901 predicted that the automobile would only be good for raising flowers in. By 1905, he predicted that the automobile would be replaced by an airship.

𝕏 | DON'T FIDDLE WITH THIS ITEM

There is a common notion that Nero fiddled while Rome burned. Another mistaken notion. The "fiddle" was not even invented until a century after Nero's death.

❧ | DOES DAN RATHER KNOW THIS?

Many people believe that the word NEWS is formed from the initial letters of the points of the compass: North, East, West, & South. NEWS does come from all different directions of the world, but the word itself comes from the Latin *novum,* which means "a new thing." If it's not new, it's not news.

*

"Mrs. Martha Johnson, a divorcée, told police that she did not think the linen with which her fiance, Daniel Manella, 31, was filling her hope chest, was all that it should be. Officers discovered that it bore the stamp of the Y.M.C.A. and arrested Manella, who, they said, confessed he stole it."

Chicago Daily News (March 8, 1931)

❧ | AN EYE FOR AN EYE, ETC.

Ed Stanley of Weed Heights, Nevada, may be the only person in the world who has ever been shot by a deer! In 1956, he was out hunting in the woods and shot a deer. As he went to the stricken animal to examine it, the deer kicked out one of its legs. The deer's leg hit Stanley's rifle, the rifle went off, and the hunter was wounded in the knee.

Source: National Safety Council

53

The $15,495 check looked impressive, so a Knoxville, Tenn. insurance broker tried to cash it. After some discussion, his bank refused to honor it. "For one thing, the numbers on the check looked all wrong," explained a cashier. "Also, we just don't cash checks that large."

Good thing, for the check was a hoax, and a hoax that may linger. Fidelity Bankers Life Insurance Co. of Richmond, Virginia, mailed 10,000 identical checks as a promotion to insurance brokers across the country. Fidelity executives, however, failed to catch a printer's error: failure to include the necessary small print "non-negotiable."

"Obviously we're embarrassed," said a Fidelity executive.

National Observer (March 11, 1968)

✿ | YOU ARE THERE (ALMOST)

The name Akutan (of the Akutan Islands in Alaska) means, "I made a mistake." The Islands received their name through an error made by the Russians.

*

Rio de Janeiro received its name because of a mistake. When a Portuguese crew sailed into Guanabara Bay on New Year's Day in 1502, the navigator assumed—mistakenly—that he had reached the mouth of a river, and hence named his discovery, Rio de Janeiro, which means "River of January."

✥ | FOUR CENTS DOESN'T GO AS FAR AS IT USED TO

In 1935, it cost a nickel to ride the subways in New York City. In that year, Mrs. Mildred Auerbach of Brooklyn attempted to get through a subway turnstile by depositing a penny instead of a nickel. She was apprehended. In her purse she carried $700 in cash and she had a bank book which showed that she had $5,000 on deposit.

Mrs. Auerbach was arrested and the story appeared in newspapers and magazines. Her husband, upon reading about it, learned for the first time how much money his wife had in the bank. He withdrew $4,000 from the account and disappeared.

Mrs. Auerbach had been collecting relief money. When the Veteran's Bureau learned about her savings, they forced her to repay $1,200.

The judge fined her $10.00.

Thus, Mrs. Auerbach's attempt to save four cents on a subway fare ended up costing her $5,210.

➤ | LOOSE LIPS SINK SIPS

"In Sacramento, California, Frank Taylor sat down in a restaurant to drink a cup of coffee. The coffee was too hot for Taylor; when he choked on it, his false teeth turned crosswise in his mouth and cut his lip. Unnerved, he fell off his chair, struck his head against a table and cut his ear. He wound up in the hospital, and was treated for bruises and lacerations."

Pageant (June, 1947)

➤ | A BIRDIE IN THE HAND IS WORTH TWO IN THE MOUTH

"The talk of the '77 Talk Tournament turned out to be a mouthful for Doris Stewart. On the final hole, Jo Anne Carner shanked a shot into the crowd. The ball struck Mrs. Stewart in the mouth, ricocheted onto the green, and landed only two feet from the pin. Carner sank the shot for a birdie and, after making sure Mrs. Stewart was not seriously injured, happily accepted the $15,000 winner's check. Never look a gift birdie in the mouth."

Woman's Sports (September, 1977)

✣ | SOME PAINTERS ARE ALL THUMBS

In Jean Leon Gerome's famous painting of the Roman gladiator—*Police Verso*—the artist has the Roman crowd pointing their thumbs down to indicate that they desire the loser to die.

However, the thumbs-down gesture did not indicate death. When the crowd wanted a gladiator to die they pointed their thumbs up or hid their thumbs inside their hands. In fact, until Gerome's painting, to turn the thumbs down was considered a favorable gesture, one that showed favor to a person.

✣ | CACHES TO ASHES

In June, 1948, a 72-year-old fruit dealer named Jerry Nikonly turned on the kitchen gas stove to heat his home, but, alas, he had quite forgotten that he had hid $1,000 in bills inside the oven. By the time Mr. Nikonly remembered, only the ashes remained.

❧ | FIT TO BE DYED

In 1856, a young English lad named William H. Perkin was attempting to produce quinine in his home laboratory. When he added oxygen to aniline oil, a tar-like mass began to accumulate in the bottom of his flask.

Perkin decided to clean his flask out with alcohol, but when he added the alcohol, the black ingredients in the flask began to change color. The young chemist quickly dipped some white silk into the mixture, and when he withdrew the material, the silk had been dyed a reddish purple.

The first synthetic dye was created, and Perkin named his dye mauve.

❧ | EVEN THE EMINENT SAMUEL JOHNSON MADE MISTAKES

Samuel Johnson thought that the word *Antimony* (a silver-white metallic element) was derived from the Greek roots, *antimonachos*, meaning "To be opposed to Monks." Actually the word is derived from the Latin *antimonium*.

⚑ | WRONG WAY CORRIGAN

In 1939, Douglas Corrigan got into his plane in New York. His destination was to have been Los Angeles, California. Unfortunately Mr. Corrigan made a wrong turn and ended up in Dublin, Ireland. He told reporters:

> I took off from New York early Sunday with the intention of flying back to Los Angeles without a stop . . . I had to go above the clouds. I was flying at 6,000 feet most of the time. I thought I was heading for California. After 25 hours I decided to descend . . . The mountains didn't look like California . . . I had only 30 gallons of fuel remaining . . . I used 290 gallons at 24 cents a gallon. That's $69.60.

🐾 | WHAT'S IN A NAME?

William Cody was the real name of "Buffalo Bill." Unfortunately, William Cody should have been called "Bison Bill," for he killed bison *not* buffalo. Although the American Bison (*Bison Americanus*) is commonly referred to as a buffalo, it really is not a true buffalo at all. In fact the American Bison is related to the ox family.

⚑ | COLUMBUS WAS AN INDIAN-GIVER

When Columbus landed in the New World, he called the inhabitants there Indians, because he thought he had landed in the East Indies. We have referred to those early inhabitants as Indians ever since, although they are not from India at all.

⚑ | AM I BLUE?

Middletown, Connecticut. May 6, 1904—Mrs. Hallock prepared a big tub of bluing for washing. While she was hanging up her clothes to dry her little daughter fell into the tub. The mother rescued the child, but no amount of rubbing would bring back her natural color as the indigo was thoroughly soaked in. It will be some time before she can go into society.

New York Times

Orono, Maine. November, 1949—Dr. W. H. Stan, head of the University of Maine's Romance Language Department ordered 20 copies of Victor Hugo's book *Notre Dame de Paris* for a French Literature class.

The order came through recently. Neatly boxed were twenty volumes of *Notre Dame: The T Formation.*

65

Water Pure, Faces Red

Washington, D.C. (UPI)—Embarrassed State Department officials said yesterday that the water supply in the United States Embassy in Moscow is not contaminated—that the department apparently was misled by some dirty test tubes.

Earlier this week, the department said tests of the water supply at the embassy had shown higher than normal traces of mercury and cyanide.

New York Daily News (January 19, 1977)

✄ | A SNAPPY TALE OF LOST TEETH

Denver, Colorado. (UPI)—It may not be the most obvious place to look, but officials have advised people who have lost their dentures to try the Public Works Department's Waste Water Division.

Division spokesman Don Fredericks said an average of 10 to 25 sets of dentures are found each year trapped on refuse-screen rakes. In 1972, he said, the division had 150 sets of dentures which would have cost their owners a total of more than $75,000.

One set of dentures, with a bullet between the teeth, was mounted by workers and given the caption, "Decisions, decisions, decisions."

New York Daily News (January 20, 1977)

❧ | *WHEN* ARE YOU PUTTING IN FOR VACATION?

Bill Maupin of Tucson, Arizona, predicted that on Sunday, June 28, 1981, he and his followers would rise up to heaven "like a bunch of balloons loose with helium." He also predicted that anyone who did not rise up to heaven on that date would face the fury of the anti-Christ, who will rule from December 2, 1984, to May 14, 1988.

A BRIDGE OVER TROUBLED WATERS?

**Nebraska Still Waits for River
To Flow Under $1,970,000 Bridge**

Decatur, Nebraska. February 4, 1952 (UPI)—Nebraskans are waiting for a congressional appropriation or an act of God to make the Missouri River flow under their new $1,970,000 bridge.

The bridge spans nothing but dry land.

Burt County, Nebraska, built the bridge in 1950, and it's all ready, toll house and all, for the first auto to cross, except that it ends on the east side where the river begins.

Almost forgotten in the last year, the bridge got back into the news when Senator Gillette (Dem.) Iowa, asked President Truman to release some $4,000,-000 which he said was earmarked for changing the Missouri River channel. Truman promised to look into the matter.

Gillette was interested in the welfare of Onawa, Iowa, which should be across the bridge from Decatur but isn't.

Originally, the river ran where it should—right under where the bridge is now. In 1946, however, the Missouri meandered off into Iowa.

Burt County officials saw a chance to save some $4,000,000 by building the bridge over dry land. They went ahead on the assurance of Army engineers that the river channel would be restored when the span was finished.

Since then the bridge has spanned bone-dry land while the river has widened the gap by moving farther into Iowa.

Army engineers estimate it will take more than Gillette's $4,000,000 to bring the Missouri back now. They put the cost at $7,900,000. Colonel H. J. Hoefer, Omaha District Army Engineer, said his office has no funds to undertake the project which he said would require work on the channel as far as sixteen miles upstream.

"It's meandering all over," Hoefer said. "We'd like to get it back, but we can't."

✖ | A ROSE BY ANY OTHER NAME DEPARTMENT

The buttercup looks like a very harmless flower, but the historian Pliny believed that if a person ate the petals of the yellow flower he or she would be seized by fits of uncontrollable laughter. Pliny was wrong.

[Pity.]

✥ | THE DOUGHNUT RECIPE THAT CHANGED AN ELECTION

**Wife's Doughnut Recipe Cost Him Nebraska
In '40 Says Vandenberg**

Omaha, Nebraska. April 13, 1948—Senator Arthur H. Vandenberg, dark horse in today's presidental primary, blames his wife's doughnut recipe for his having lost the 1940 Nebraska primary to Governor Thomas E. Dewey.

Mrs. Vandenberg is known among her friends as an excellent cook. Her recipe for doughnuts is listed in the Senate cookbook. Senator Hugh Buttons says he never tasted a better doughnut.

In 1940, the Vandenberg-for-President-Committee in Nebraska scheduled 600 tea parties for farm wives. Printed invitations were sent out in the shape of a doughnut with a hole in the middle. On the back of the invitation was printed Mrs. Vandenberg's famous doughnut recipe.

Dairy farmers who make a living off butter, and hog farmers with lard to sell, took a look at the recipe and turned red. Mrs. Vandenberg's recipe called for neither butter nor lard; she uses Crisco instead.

To this day, Senator Vandenberg figures his wife's recipe cost him the farm vote.

St. Louis Post-Dispatch

⚓ | DELUSIONS OF GRANDEUR

Magician

In St. Paul, Robert Heger invited friends to a performance of the Hindu rope trick, most baffling of magical feats. On a dimly lighted stage a coil of rope stiffened at Heger's command, rose slowly into the air. A Hindu boy clambered up the rope, and vanished. Armed with a sabre, a second Hindu swarmed up after him, tossed down arms, legs, head, and torso. Finally, Magician Heger enfolded the bloody members in his robe, then opened it for the Hindu lad to step forth.

Delighted at his success, Magician Heger proposed to go to England and collect the $25,000 prize offered by the Magic Circle Society of Magicians in London for the successful performance of the trick. Next afternoon he stepped onto the stage again. Excited, he forgot to have the lights dimmed, began to mutter mystically in the glare of a white spotlight. The audience saw a thin bright wire hoist the rope aloft, saw the Hindu boy climb up, and hop easily behind a curtain. When the bloody members thudded down and the magician picked them up, the audience tittered to see an arm left oozing on the stage after the whole boy had re-appeared. Magician Heger announced that he would not go to London.

Time (November, 1931)

⚜ | A FISH BY ANY OTHER NAME, ETC.

The black bass is not a bass—it is a sunfish
The white perch is not a perch—it is a bass.
The rock-bass is not a bass—it is a sunfish.
The wall-eyed pike is not a pike—it is a perch.

What else do all the above fish have in common? They all grow larger during the time they are caught and the time a fisherman describes the catch to his friend.

❧ | A MISTAKE THAT BURNS US UP

In 1942, United Artists released a film entitled *I Married a Witch*. The film featured Veronica Lake and Frederic March, and opened with a scene showing a witch in seventeenth-century Massachusetts being burned at the stake.

Witches were not burned at the stake in Puritan New England. In fact, there is no record of a single witch being burned to death in seventeenth-century New England. They were crushed to death, stoned, or drowned.

❧ | HOW'S THAT AGAIN?

There was a law in the state of Kansas that read:

> "When two trains approach each other at a crossing, they shall both come to a full stop, and neither shall start up until the other has gone."

♟ | HOW NOT TO ESCAPE FROM PRISON

And how about a round of applause for Kerin Hughes, age twenty-one. In July 1981, Mr. Hughes managed to escape from New Hampshire's State Prison. Several miles from the prison, Mr. Hughes got lost. He spotted some men playing softball and decided to ask one of them for directions to Highway I-93. Unfortunately, the softball players were police recruits, and the man Hughes singled out for advice was none other than the commandant of the New Hampshire Training Academy. The commandant, Robert Bossey, hailed a passing state trooper, and Mr. Hughes was whisked back to prison.

⚐ | DOMESTIC BLISS?

"In Sand Lake, Michigan, John W. Vos, suddenly remembering that he had not kissed his wife goodbye, turned back, and collided with a car driven by his wife rushing to overtake him."

Time (October 4, 1948)

⚐ | DOMESTIC HISS?

Although the White House officially released the news that First Lady Nancy Reagan had been born in 1923, a birth certificate located by NBC television states that Mrs. Reagan was born in 1921.

✈ | PARACHUTIST FALLS 3,500 FEET, LIVES

Canton, Ohio. (AP)—A man who survived a 3,500-foot plunge after his parachute failed to open completely says he was spared because he didn't panic and "the good Lord had a hand between me and the ground."

But Albert Lewis of Columbus also said he had prepared himself for death when both of his parachutes failed while he was skydiving on June 28.

Despite the close call, the 33-year-old electrician says he intends to resume parachuting.

"All the way down, my only concern was untangling my chute. But try as I might, it was no use. I knew this was the end," Lewis said at Timken Mercy Medical Center, where he is recovering from a broken ankle, broken left thigh bone, two broken vertebrae and various bruises.

Lewis, a member of the Canton Parachute Club and the U.S. Army Reserve, said he had made 23 jumps since he began parachuting in 1973.

He said the accident "was just one of those things you have no control over."

After jumping from the plane, he said he pulled the ripcord and looked up to see whether the chute opened fully.

"Only about a fifth of the canopy opened and it just fluttered over my head," he said.

He then used his emergency chute, but it became tangled in the main chute.

"I was totally engrossed with correcting the malfunction. I tried and tried to pull the reserve chute out of the entanglement until I knew it was no use," he said. "I have given up. I knew this must be it. But fortunately, the good Lord had a hand between me and the ground.

"The next thing I knew, I hit the ground. It was a tremendous shock. I was hurt, but I never lost consciousness."

Lewis said he joked with paramedics who rushed to his aid.

"I didn't want them to cut my T-shirt off, and I told them about it. It's a special shirt, the one I always wear when I jump," he said.

He said the accident was "part of the risk that is built into the sport. As soon as I'm able, I plan to try it again."

✖ | SOME DAYS NOTHING GOES RIGHT

In 1956, a farmer in Las Vegas, Nevada, decided to get rid of a gopher by dropping a small bomb down the gopher hole. The gopher took one look at the small bomb rolling toward him and immediately pushed it back out of the hole. The farmer panicked, picked up the bomb, and gave it a good toss. The bomb landed near his barn, and twelve tons of hay were destroyed by fire.

Source: National Safety Council

81

✌ | MALPRACTICE MAKES PERFECT

Let's hear it for the two surgeons who, in 1981, went into the operating room to correct a birth defect on the leg of a nine-year-old boy. The boy was suffering from Blount's Disease, in which bones are improperly fused. The surgeons, unfortunately, made one slight error: they operated on the boy's good leg.

✠ | HER POSTCARD GOT A REAL RIDE FOR 4¢

West Warwick, Rhode Island. (UPI)—When Rita Duhamel reached into her mailbox last week, she found a postcard carrying Abraham Lincoln's violet profile on a 4-cent stamp.

Addressed to her daughter, the postcard was mailed on July 15, 1964, from Brunswick, Maine.

Nobody knows where it had been for fifteen years.

The card had been sent by Sherry Humes who at the time was fourteen years old.

✥ | PROPHET PREDICTS THE END OF THE WORLD

Frankfurt, Germany. April 1, 1950 (AP)—Johannes Lang's prophecy seems to have gone askew.

The 50-year-old German predicted March 18 that World War III would begin on April 1, 1950, with an attack on the West by Russia. He said that both he and Stalin studied the French seer Nostradamus, and that Stalin was all geared for an April 1st push.

The German prophet was not available for comment.

*

And then there was the restaurant in Chicago that featured its specialty of the day: Dreaded Veal Cutlets.

85

⚑ | LONGFELLOW'S MISTAKE

In his poem, "Paul Revere's Ride," (one of the stories in *Tales of a Wayside Inn*), Longfellow wrote:

> *It was two by the village clock,*
> *When he came to the bridge in Concord town.*
> *He heard the bleating of the flock,*
> *And the twitter of birds among the trees,*
> *And felt the breath of morning breeze*
> *Blowing over the meadows brown. . . .*

Actually, Paul Revere, on the night of his famous ride, never reached Concord. At one A.M. William Dawes, Dr. Samuel Prescott, and Paul Revere set out toward Concord to warn the citizens of the approach of British troops. Unfortunately, the three men rode into the path of a British cavalry patrol, and although Dawes and Prescott managed to escape, Paul Revere was captured. Dr. Prescott finally rode on to Concord, but Paul Revere, alas, did not.

✺ | IS MY STATE RED DEPARTMENT

The state of Rhode Island might well have received its name because of a mistake. In 1524, the Italian explorer Giovanni da Verrazano reported that he had seen an island "in size about equal to the Island of Rhodes." Verrazano was most likely referring to Block Island, but the name became attached to the island where Newport stands. In the mid-seventeenth century, Newport's town fathers decided that "this island, commonly called Aquidneck, shall be from henceforth called the Isle of Rhodes, or Rhode Island."

Actually the official name of America's smallest state is "Rhode Island and Providence Plantations."

✌ | YOUNGSTERS DIAL SANTA, GET MORTUARY ON LINE

Mendon, Illinois. (UPI)—Many Central Illinois youngsters trying to call Santa Claus are getting quite a shock this season.

They get the Curry Funeral Home in Mendon.

"Can you imagine how your heart would fall when you thought you'd dialed Santa Claus and someone answered, 'Curry Funeral Home'?" Georgia Curry asked.

Since Thanksgiving, Chicago radio stations have been broadcasting an Illinois Bell Telephone Co. promotion urging children to call Santa at the Chicago number 312-936-2525.

Unfortunately, many youngsters in the 217 area code in Central Illinois fail to note that the number is in Chicago and just dial 936-2525. They get the mortuary in Mendon, twelve miles northeast of Quincy.

Mrs. Curry and her husband, Eugene, who operate the funeral home, have been answering at least a dozen calls a day for Santa from children from all over the state.

On the day after Thanksgiving, when the promotion started, they received an estimated fifty calls.

The mixup was reported by Paul Colgan of the *Quincy Herald-Whig.*

89

Mary Jane Bradley-Smith, who is handling the promotion for Illinois Bell, said radio and newspaper ads have been changed to emphasize that the number is in Chicago.

When children do get the right number, they hear a recording of a jolly Santa Claus saying Mrs. Santa Claus will come on the line to answer their requests. The correct Chicago number is reported to be averaging more than 30,000 calls a day.

🐝 | GREAT MOMENTS IN THE THEATER #1

Actor Has Verve, Fire, Dash . . .
and a Bee in His Wig

There was true theatrical fire and dash in the performance of Edwin Steffe as he stepped on stage at Municipal Opera Monday Night as Baron Vilmos in the current production, *Venus in Silk.*

The added verve was supplied by a bumble bee that had taken up residence in Steffe's wig. The actor, late for his cue, had slapped on the wig hurriedly as he made his entrance. The bee sat down—hard.

After finishing his opening appearance, Steffe dashed into the wings, ears ringing with applause or the effects of the sting, and pulled off the wig. The bee was dead.

A fellow actor, using tweezers, removed the stinger from Steffe's scalp.

"Certainly gave point to my performance," Steffe remarked.

St. Louis Post-Dispatch (June 16, 1948)

✵ | IS MY NOSE RED DEPARTMENT (Not you, Rudolph)

When Anne Morrow Lindbergh was a little girl, J. P. Morgan, the elder, was coming to tea at the Dwight Morrows'. Fearing the frankness of childhood, Mrs. Morrow talked to Anne beforehand.

"I need not tell you," she said, "that it is rude to comment on anything peculiar about people you meet, so, of course, if you notice that Mr. Morgan's nose is different you won't say anything about it."

Upon meeting the famous guest Anne fixed her eyes relentlessly on the celebrated nose. Her mother noticed this with trepidation and tried, not too obviously, to speed her departure. At last the child was gone—safely gone.

Mrs. Morrow breathed a sigh of relief and, pouring a cup of tea, she asked her visitor with a new complacence, "And now, Mr. Morgan, will you have cream or lemon in your nose?"

Reader's Digest (1949)

✈ | DAY BEGAN WITH 'A BUMMER,' AND GOT WORSE

Provo, Utah. (AP)—Brian Heise had the kind of Fourth of July people dream about—in nightmares.

The 30-year-old Brigham Young University student says that after his series of little calamities, he can't help wondering if "God wanted me dead, but just kept missing."

It began the instant he woke up that day.

"I heard this tinkle-tinkle, and I thought, 'What a bummer! It's raining on the Fourth of July.' Then I realized it wasn't raining outside; it was raining inside."

Water from a ruptured water pipe in a neighbor's apartment above was pouring from the cupboards and electrical outlets in Heise's apartment.

He called the building manager, and the manager told him to rent some cleaning equipment.

"So I went out to my car to get the equipment and I had a flat tire," Heise said.

After changing the tire, he decided to call a friend to help him with the cleanup. He went back inside, picked up the phone and was zapped by an electric shock.

"When I jumped back," he added, "the phone fell off the wall."

He tried to get out to his car again, but the flooding had caused the bricks in his apartment walls to shift, making it impossible to open the front door.

Heise began screaming out the window, and a neighbor came and kicked in the door.

Opening the door, Heise could see his car had been stolen.

He located the auto a few minutes later in a nearby parking lot. He pushed it to a gas station, filled it up, and he and a friend finally found a water-sucking machine to use on his apartment.

Heise, a member of a Civil War nostalgia group, was scheduled to march in Provo's Freedom Festival parade that morning. But when he pulled on his uniform and went outside, he found a parade float blocking his driveway.

After searching unsuccessfully for the float's driver, Heise had to give up.

That evening, Heise participated—without incident—in a mock Civil War battle at BYU's football stadium. But when he returned to his seat he sat on his bayonet, which "sank in several inches," he said.

Heise and some friends tried to find a doctor, but got stuck in a post-performance traffic jam.

He finally walked to a clinic, where a doctor patched him up and gave him a ride back to his car.

When he got back home, Heise, a canary breeder, discovered that part of his ceiling had fallen, killing four of his birds.

Even after Heise made it through the day alive, his bad luck persisted. While he waited for his landlord to arrange a cleaning crew to pull up his water-soaked carpet, he contracted a skin rash which soon covered his legs. His doctor said the rash was caused by the mold on the carpet.

And last Wednesday, he slipped on the wet carpet and badly bruised his tailbone.

"They say turn the other cheek," he said, "but I only have one left to sit on."

The Morning Union (July 13, 1981)

☂ | THE DAY HARRY S. TRUMAN CONFUSED THEODORE ROOSEVELT WITH FRANKLIN DELANO

In a speech at Jefferson-Jackson Day Dinner, held on February 19, 1948, in Washington D.C., President Harry S. Truman stated that he would stick to "the politics of Thomas Jefferson, Andrew Jackson, Woodrow Wilson, and Theodore Roosevelt."

"Although Truman apparently meant to say 'Franklin Roosevelt," he smilingly refused to correct his remark. When questioned about his slip of the tongue, Truman said, "Theodore Roosevelt belongs in the same class with Franklin. We admit all liberals."

In a local election in the Corte district on the island of Corsica, 4,303 registered voters cast 9,647 votes in an election.

✒ | REDUCE THAT SEDUCING

Newspapers have often committed misprints, but one of the more memorable lapses occurred when the *St. Louis Globe-Democrat* reprinted the following item from a Hedda Hopper column:

> Kathryn Grayson had better begin seducing if she wishes to wear that wedding dress she had fitted a couple of months ago.

✍ | THEY HIT YOU WHERE YOU LIVE DEPT.

Chester, Pennsylvania. June 17, 1949 (AP)—John McCafferty, 46, arrested as a vagrant, insisted that the police were wrong. He said he had a home and gave its address: 714 McIlvane Street. Today, McCafferty came before Magistrate R. Robinson Lowry. "Where did you get that address?" the magistrate asked. "It's just an address," the defendant replied. "I'll say it is," agreed the Magistrate. "That's where I live. Ninety days."

*

Aurora, Illinois. Handed a batch of subpoenas to serve, Police Lt. George N. Rees couldn't locate one of the persons wanted as a witness—a Rees Geon. Finally he took the summons to court and explained his troubles. "You're it," he was told. "That's Rees, Geo. N."

Newsweek (May 8, 1939)

✢ | WHERE WAS TELEVISION IN 1910?

Persons who answer questions sent in by readers often make mistakes. For example, when an Agnes Moorehead fan wrote to the *Honolulu Star-Bulletin & Advertiser* to inquire about the date of Ms. Moorehead's death, the newspaper supplied the following information:

> Agnes Moorehead died on May 1, 1974, at age sixty-seven. The actress made her first professional appearance when three years old, singing on a television program sponsored by her father, a minister.

‚ì∏‚ì∏ | ·STAMP OUT MISTAKES

When noted counterfeiter of rare stamps, Juan De Sperati, produced copies of the famous 10-Cent Rose and T-E-N stamps of the United States Confederacy, Mr. Sperati made a slight error. He used a Middlebury, Vermont, handstamp to cancel them.

*

"In Detroit, tireless burglar John Fabian, after creeping through seven floors of hotel corridors in search of an unlocked door, finally found one on the 210th try, walked straight into a darkened room and the clutches of its three wakeful occupants: an FBI agent and 2 cops."

Time (March 31, 1947)

⚑ | SHE SHOULD HAVE TRIED THE GETTYSBURG ADDRESS

When a woman in Harbor Beach, Michigan, sent a letter to President Reagan, she sent her letter to Reagan's Los Angeles campaign headquarters at 9841 Airport Road. Her letter even had a correct zip code, and still it was returned to her, stamped RETURN TO SENDER: MOVED, LEFT NO ADDRESS.

⚑ | DEMOCRATS MADE MISTAKES, TOO

During a Democratic Party National Telethon telecast, Jackie Cooper told millions of viewers that, "The twin cities of St. Paul and Minneapolis are in Michigan."

✈ | A LITTLE PICK-ME-UP

"In Manhattan, Arthur Crayton tried to pick the pocket of a fat man asleep in a subway station, got his hand caught firmly when the sleeper shifted, was finally extricated by two cops."

Time (February 17, 1947)

*

"In Duston, England, Marmaduke Harrison, aged eighty-two, died after breaking a thigh while trying to put both feet in the same trouser leg."

Time (April 5, 1937)

103

❧ | WHATTA PICCADILLY OF A BASH!

London (AP)—The party at the Sundown Club early yesterday was a doozie. It had six runaway snakes, a trick marksman who shot a disc jockey by mistake and some girl fire eaters who were almost seriously burned.

It was all in fun, really, to celebrate the stage opening of "Tommy," the rock musical recorded by the British group The Who and later made into a movie.

Cowboy Bill Coady, the trick shooter, was supposed to be the big attraction at the club in London's West End. He was shooting balloons behind him, using a mirror to aim.

"Suddenly he seemed to miss everything—except disc jockey Gerry Collins, who was inside his wooden stand," said club spokesman Chris Moore. "I think he was using a .22 air rifle."

Collins, 30, slumped to the floor moaning "I've been shot" into the loudspeakers. He was taken to the hospital, where he was said to be not seriously hurt. Collins was hit in the side.

Disaster struck again when the fire eaters' inflammable liquid was lit. A stagehand grabbed it and made for the exit but was tripped up. "It was like a fireball set off in the corridor," said Moore.

Then, as guests and firemen tried to douse the flames, the snakes used by Dahli, a snake charmer, tried to escape from their basket.

A rescue attempt was mounted by Dahli, but as the club general manager, Ian Baxter remarked, "There weren't many people who would go near them." All were finally rounded up.

Smoke from the fire began to seep into the dance hall, but the party went on. "They all thought the smoke was part of our special effects," said Baxter.

The party ended happily, with most of the guests still unaware of the shooting, the fire, and the snakes. And the firemen finished by dancing with the guests.

New York Daily News (February 8, 1979)

✒ | PRESIDENT, IN SPEECH 'SLIPS' OUT OF OFFICE

Washington, D.C. February 10 (AP)—President Carter, in a slip of the tongue, referred to himself today as "a former President."

He made the slip when he was telling several hundred Federal employees that government officials often think they have resolved a problem when a law is passed or an administrative action is taken.

"As a former President, I know that that is not the fact," Mr. Carter said.

Presumably, he was referring to his former position as Governor of Georgia.

New York Times (February 11, 1978)

✺ | MR. McCARTHY LEARNS
IT'S JUST A MATTER OF CHOICE

When Callahan Richard McCarthy of Waterville, Maine, wrote "none" for his second choice for letters on his auto-license plates, he meant he had no second choice. He wanted his initials—CRM.

After two months of waiting, he received the bright mustard-yellow plates. His first choice was not available. On his plates appeared what state authorities thought was his second choice, NONE.

National Observer (January 29, 1968)

✺ | SORRY

Yesterday's "How to save your life" article said to give heart attack victims cardiopulmonary chest thrusts at the rate of six times a minute. A zero was left out. It should have read "60 times a minute."

BOY'S RARE AILMENT REVEALS 13-YEAR-OLD MIXUP OF NEWBORNS

Richmond, California. November 27 (AP)—When doctors decided 13-year-old Efren de Loa needed a bone-marrow transplant and went looking for a donor, they discovered he was unrelated to his parents, brothers, and sisters.

They uncovered a maternity-ward mixup, tracked down what apparently is his natural family and staged a reunion—and now they hope to find a suitable donor.

Efren and his family flew to his birthplace in Mexicali, Mexico, last weekend to meet his natural family and to arrange for the transplants he needs to survive, the *San Francisco Chronicle* reported today.

Officials said they will not be certain they have found the right family until compatibility tests are completed this week at the University of California at Los Angeles, where the family of Mauricio and Margarita Montes went for testing.

If the tests show the Monteses are Efren's natural parents, the transplant operation could be done next month, doctors said.

Until doctors diagnosed the rare blood disease that required a bone-marrow transplant from a brother or sister, Efren and his family had no idea a mixup had occurred when he was born.

The doctors ran tests on family members, trying to find the best possible donor. They quickly learned than Efren was not related to the De Loa family.

Eventually, reports in the newspaper La Voz de la Frontera reached the Montes family in Mexico. The two mothers recognized each other when they met and recalled they had given birth at the same time at the same hosital.

The mixup occurred, officials said, when the newborn baby boys were placed in the same hospital crib without name tags.

There are no plans to switch the boys back to their natural parents. "I saw him grow. I raised him and he stays with me," Montes said of the boy he thought was his son.

The De Loas moved from Mexicali to Richmond in 1972. Last year, doctors diagnosed Efren's illness as aplastic anemia, a disease in which the bone marrow, which produces blood cells, stops working.

The chances of the boy's survival will increase from about 15 percent to 60 percent with the bone-marrow transplants, doctors said.

♞ | WE OFTEN MAKE MISTAKES IN MATING

If you ever play a game of chess and lose in two moves, you know you have made a bad mistake. In fact, you have fallen into what is commonly called a fool's mate. To lose in two moves, you and your opponent must make the following plays:

WHITE	BLACK
1. Pawn—King Bishop 3	Pawn to King 4
2. Pawn—King's Knight 4	Queen to Rook 5 (MATE)

⚑ | PAINTING MISTAKE #456,890

In one of America's most famous patriotic masterpieces—*The Spirit of '76*, painted by Archibald M. Willard—the flag shown, consisting of thirteen stars arranged in a circle on a blue field, and thirteen stripes, alternating red and white, was not approved by Congress until June 14, 1777.

⚔ | BUNKER HILL MISTAKE

One of the more famous mistakes in American history is based upon the notion that the Battle of Bunker Hill was actually fought at Bunker Hill. The truth of the matter is that this famous battle of the American Revolution, fought on June 16, 1775, was fought on Breed's Hill some 2,000 feet away. In Charlestown, Massachusetts, the Bunker Hill monument is located on Breed's Hill.

🏴 | YES, BUT DID SHE DROP A STITCH?

Oswestry, England. October 4 (UPI)—After performing surgery on Jane Vaughan, aged eighty-two, the doctor asked if she had lost a six-inch knitting needle.

That's what he found lodged in her back. The doctor said he believed Mrs. Vaughan sat on it without noticing about a year ago.

🏴 | ELEPHANT'S TOSSED SALAD

Newbury Park, California. (AP)—The sanitation-men knew they were in trouble when their truck lost its brakes going downhill, but they never suspected that the real threat of injury would come from an enraged elephant.

No one was hurt when their garbage truck knocked down a high voltage line and a telephone pole and finally tipped over in Tony Gentry's front yard here. The trouble started when Gentry's pet Burmese elephant, apparently upset by all the commotion, started picking up rocks and throwing them at the astonished crew.

The fusillade didn't stop by the time an electric company crew arrived to fix the downed power line, so the owner was consulted on how to best pacify the pachyderm. Gentry, a former circusman, recommended a watermelon.

The elephant, Burma Mountain Gypsy, stopped chucking rocks long enough to eat the melon they threw her. Then she threw the rind at them. There were no injuries.

(September 24, 1976)

📰 | CLASSIC NEWSPAPER HEADLINES

NOTED ISTANBUL MOSQUITOES
BECOME PUBLIC LIBRARIES
(*Wilson, North Carolina, 1934*)

FIFTY DEAD PERSONS
HEAR MUSIC PROGRAM
(*Indianapolis, Indiana*)

SANTA ROSA MAN DENIES
HE COMMITTED SUICIDE
IN SOUTH SAN FRANCISCO
(*Burlington, California*)

✣ | GREAT MOMENTS IN THE THEATER, #2

Let us have a moment of silence for the poor actor who appeared in *Richard III* by William Shakespeare. In Act I of that play, the actor was to deliver the line, "My lord, stand back and let the coffin pass."

Unfortunately, the line came out as follows: "My Lord, stand back, and let the parson cough."

✣ | THE STRAWBERRY MISTAKE

The word *strawberry* really has nothing to do with straw. We call the fruit a strawberry because of a corruption in pronunciation. The fruit takes its name from strayberry because it grows on a plant whose roots stray in all directions.

✵ | RIB MISTAKE

In Chapter Two of *Genesis* it is written that woman was created from Adam's rib:

> And the Lord God caused a deep sleep to fall upon Adam,
> and he slept; and he took one of his ribs,
> and closed up the flesh instead thereof;
> And the rib, which the Lord God had taken from man,
> made he a woman, and brought her unto the man.

Because of the above passage, many persons believe that a man has one less set of ribs than a woman. Alas, such persons are in error. Both men and women have the same number of ribs: twelve on each side.

✵ | TIME FLIES?

The Greek poet Hesiod once stated that the average crow lives to be over 2,500 years old. Now *that's* a mistake.

And then there's the famous mistakes the post-office makes. For example, there is the 24¢ airmail stamp that shows the airplane flying upside down.

However, this mistake paid off. The upside-down airmail stamp is now worth at least $135,000.

🏴 | HELP YOURSELF TO A SPOONFUL

Former Army Major Robert R. Spooner, of Colorado Springs, once introduced himself by saying, "Okay, fellows, this is Major Speaner spooking."

Was it only coincidence that such a spoonerism should be committed by a person named Spooner?

⚑ | I'D RATHER BE RIGHT—OH, FORGET IT

In 1943, James C. McMullin wrote an article for a publication entitled *Prediction of Things to Come.* In his article, Mr. McMullin wrote:

> "The author hereby sticks his neck out to predict that Mr. [Wendell] Willkie will be elected President of the United States some day; in 1948, or 1952, if not in 1944."

✌ | REMEMBER (Classic Schoolroom Boners):

1. Gladiators are things that warm up rooms.

2. The equator is a menagerie lion that runs around the earth.

3. A Republican is one of the sinners mentioned in the *Bible*.

4. The five continents are A, E, I, O, and U.

5. No queen sat on a thorn longer than Queen Victoria. She did it for more than sixty years.

In 1926, Professor A. W. Bickerton maintained that shooting a rocket to the moon would be impossible. He wrote:

> "This foolish idea of shooting at the moon is an example of the absurd length to which vicious specialization will carry scientists working in thought-tight compartments. Let us critically examine the proposal. For a projectile entirely to escape the gravitation of the earth, it needs a velocity of seven miles a second. The thermal energy of a gram at this speed is 15,180 calories. . . . The energy of our most violent explosive is less than 1,500 calories per gram. Consequently, even had the explosive nothing to carry, it has only one-tenth of the energy necessary to escape the earth. . . . Hence the proposition appears to be basically impossible."

⚑ | PAGING CAPTAIN HOOK

Topsell, in his *History of Serpents*, claims that, "The Crocodile runneth away from a man if he wink with his left eye, and look steadfastly upon him with his right eye."

In 1818, John Cleves Symmes, a former Captain in the Ohio Infantry, wrote in his book that the center of the earth was hollow and habitable:

St. Louis, Missouri Territory,
North America
April 10, A.D. 1818

To All the World:

I declare the earth is hollow and habitable within, containing a number of solid concentric spheres, one within the other, and that it is open to the poles twelve or sixteen degrees. I pledge my life in support of this truth, and am ready to explore the hollow, if the world will support and aid me in the undertaking.

John Cleves Symmes

❧ | JOHN KEATS' FAMOUS MISTAKE

In writing his great sonnet, Keats' confused Cortez with the explorer who actually discovered the Pacific Ocean—Balboa. Still, the poem survives and is considered great, in spite of the mistake:

On First Looking into Chapman's Homer

Much have I travelled in the realms of gold
*   And many goodly states and kingdoms seen;*
*   Round many western islands have I been*
Which bards in fealty to Apollo hold.
Oft of one wide expanse had I been told
*   That deep-browed Homer ruled as his demesne;*
*   Yet did I never breathe its pure serene*
Till I heard Chapman speak out loud and bold.

Then felt I like some watcher of the skies
*   When a new planet swims into his ken;*
Or like stout Cortez when with eagle eyes
*   He stared at the Pacific, and all his men*
Looked at each other with a wild surmise—
*   Silent, upon a peak in Darien.*

❧ | A BOXING MISTAKE IN LEWISTON, MAINE

On September 29, 1946, Ralph Walton was sitting in the corner of a boxing ring. He was preparing to face his opponent Al Coutre. The bell rang, signalling the beginning of the fight, and Ralph Walton began to adjust his gum shield (a piece of equipment designed to protect a fighter's gums and teeth). As he was adjusting his shield, Coutre scurried across the ring and landed a solid blow on Walton's chin. Walton went down and was counted out. The entire fight, complete with ten-second count, took ten and a half seconds.

(Some days things just don't go right.)

❧ | TO ERR IS SHAKESPEARE DEPARTMENT

In *Julius Caesar,* Shakespeare has one of his characters say, "The clock hath stricken three." Alas, there were no clocks in Julius Caesar's day.

❧ | THERE'S NO MISTAKE ABOUT IT

Murphy's Law
If something can go wrong, it will go wrong, and in the worse possible way.

✥ | EVEN PAINTERS MAKE MISTAKES

When Emanuel Gottlieb Leutze (1816–1868) created his famous painting of *Washington Crossing the Delaware,* he made a few mistakes. The boat is too small to hold all the people that are crowded inside it, and who would stand up in a rowboat? More importantly, the flag shown in the painting was not created at the time Washington made his famous crossing.

DR. BEARD, 101, READS HE'S BEEN DEAD A YEAR

Norwalk, Connecticut. May 27, 1934—Dr. Augustus Field Beard was interested but not perturbed today to discover on looking through the 1934 edition of *Beckwith's Almanac* that an important event of May 14, 1933, was the death of Dr. Augustus Field Beard, aged 100 years. Dr. Beard is 101 now. He is the oldest alumnus of Yale and the oldest Congregational minister in the country. He said he might ask Annie E. Russell of East Haven, editor of the *Almanac* out to dinner and convince her that he wasn't dead.

*

Cleveland, Ohio. June 6, 1949 (UPI)—A burglar who got so tired on the job that he crawled into bed with the victim and went to sleep was in jail here today. The captive identified himself as E. Lilly of Detroit. His snoring awakened Mrs. Matilda Besman, 82, who ran for a roomer and then called the police while the roomer watched the sleeping burglar. Police awakened him and found two diamond rings, a watch, and a necklace in his pockets. Lilly was sleeping with his hat on.

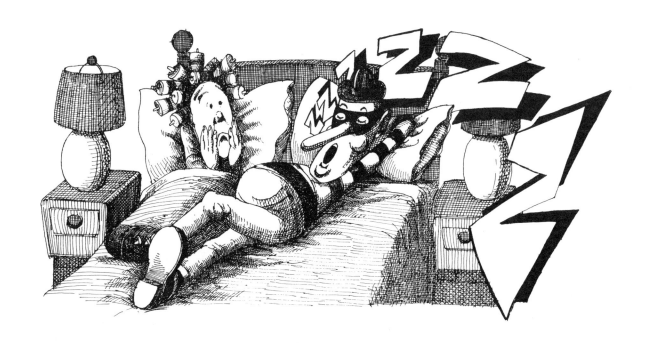

✄ | ROBERT TAFT ADMITS AN ERROR—SORT OF

Taft Admits Error on Age of Cities

April 4, 1948—Senator Robert A. Taft, called to book last night on his assertion made at City Hall yesterday, that Cincinnati was an older city than St. Louis, admitted his error. However, he said at the outset of his banquet speech:

> "I was thinking primarily of the slums of this city, which I had just seen, and those in Cincinnati. While it is true that St. Louis was founded a few years earlier than Cincinnati, it did not grow so rapidly at first, and I still believe that the slums of Cincinnati are older than those of St. Louis."

✄ | CAN'T GET AROUND MUCH ANY MORE!

In 1981, the Fire Department of Clairton, Pennsylvania purchased a long ladder truck. Unfortunately, the truck was so long that it was not able to go around fifty-six of the town's corners.

London, England. July 3, 1953 (AP)—Philip Dale, leading actor in the play *Talk of the Night* snapped on a pair of handcuffs for a comedy monologue in Act One last night, and, you guessed it.

As soon as the curtain fell, handcuffed, keyless, Dale hurried to a nearby fire station to get the things filed off.

A suspicious fireman hustled him to the Bow Street Police Station, several blocks away. The police finally satisfied themselves he wasn't a criminal and cut the cuffs loose.

He sped back to the Irvine Theater to find that the management had cancelled the performance and had given the audience tickets for another night.

*

Ex-hockey goalie Jacques Plante comments about errors: "How would you like a job where, if you make a mistake, a big red light goes on and 18,000 people boo?"

✌ | GREAT MOMENTS IN SLEEP, PART II

In August 1981, Michael Schaetzle (aged twelve) was sleeping in the back of his parents' camper while the family was driving along Highway I-20 in Alabama. Michael started to dream about swimming in Myrtle Beach. The water looked inviting, and so Michael dived in. He jumped out of the camper and landed on the highway. He was nearly run over by a trailer truck, but he escaped with only minor cuts and bruises. Michael's parents, meanwhile, didn't even realize that their son was missing until they pulled into a rest stop. They called the police, drove to the hospital, and brought their sleep-diving son safely home.

✌ | SOME MISTAKES GET OUR GOAT

Once newsman Douglas Edwards was doing a radio show in which he had planned to interview a beer brewer. The brewer brought along a pet goat as a live trademark. The radio show barely got started when the goat devoured Douglas Edwards' script.

131

⚜ | FOR ALL PERSONS WHO HAVE EVER MADE A MISTAKE

"To err is human"
Is writ upon the Philosopher's Cup.
Ah, yes, but more human it is,
After erring, to cover up.

Louis Phillips